PROPERTY DISPUTES IN INDIAN FAMILIES

HISTORICAL, PSYCHOLOGICAL AND LEGAL ASPECTS

SIVA PRASAD BOSE

This book is dedicated for all those who are involved in long running property cases within the family in Indian Courts.

Contents

Preface

Property and land disputes take up the largest proportion of cases in Indian courts. A significant number of such disputes are within families, with siblings and cousins fighting with each other. This creates an unnecessary drain on the economy and on productivity. In this book we discuss the psychology of property disputes within the family and also look at some historical property disputes in India, starting from the ancient and medieval ages.

In this book we briefly discuss the history of property disputes in India within the family. We also briefly cover the psychology of property disputes within siblings. We also discuss the laws related to property transfers and legal strategies one may take if they are caught in a property case.

CHAPTER ONE

History of Family Property Disputes in India

In this chapter we discuss the history of property disputes in India within the family.

India is no stranger to property and land disputes. We have plenty of tales from mythology and history to show that within the family in the absence of a strong heir or a clearly defined successor to the land. Usually, after the death of a patriarch, the brothers fought each other for the right to the land. However, disputes within a family are not limited to brothers and can also include other members such as uncles, or even between a father and son for control of the kingdom.

1.1 Family property disputes in Indian mythology

The ancient Indian epics Ramayana and Mahabharata speak of property disputes within joint families.

In Ramayana, king Dasharatha has 4 sons and is planning to give the kingdom to the eldest son Rama, but the mother of a younger brother Bharata wants her son to gain the kingdom, so she persuades the king to banish Rama to the forest so that her son can rule.

In Mahabharata, two groups of cousin brothers, Pandavas and Kauravas, fight a war with each other for the right to rule the kingdom. The Pandava brothers eventually win the war, but at great human cost and all the Kaurava brothers die in the war.

1.2 Family property disputes in ancient India

Fights between king Bimbisara and his son Ajatshatru of the Mauryan empire in 5th century BC is well known. There were similar fights of succession between emperor Ashoka and his brothers.

A similar rivalry is described among the king Bharata and his brother Bahubali, sons of king Rishabhanath.

1.3 Family property disputes in Mughal times

In the medieval era, India again has seen plenty of property disputes between siblings, mainly in royal houses but also among ordinary landowning people. Usually when the patriarch, such as the Mughal emperor dies, his sons start squabbling among themselves for the right to win the kingdom and this leads to a lot of bloodshed.

Famous examples include the house of the Mughal emperors: As the emperor Shah Jahan became old, he appointed one of his sons, Dara Shikoh, as the heir to the kingdom. But the other sons were not happy with this and raised armies and started fighting. Ultimately, the youngest son, Aurangzeb, won the throne and killed his brothers and even imprisoned his own father.

Previously, emperor Shah Jahan had a similar fight with his half-brother prince Khusrou and other brothers, before he could win the Mughal throne. Other mughal emperors who had sibling rivalries included emperor Humayun with his brothers Kamran, Askari and Hindal.

1.4 Family property disputes in other medieval kingdoms

In the 1100s, King Jaichand of Gahadwala dynasty and King Prithviraj Chauhan of Delhi were supposedly cousins and their rivalry is also famous by the legend of Prithviraj Raso, although its authenticity is somewhat debatable.

The Pandyan kingdom of south India in 1300s had a rivalry between brothers Vira Pandya and Sundara Pandya. As it happened, Sundara Pandya invited the Khalji rulers of Delhi to invade his brother Vira Pandya's kingdom, leading to the loss of its independence.

The Vijaynagar empire had its own share of family rivalries after Krishnadeva Raya in 1500s, notably between Rama Raya and Achyuta Deva Raya who were related.

The Maratha empire had a similar rivalry between Shivaji's son Shambhaji and his half-brother Rajaram in the 1600s. The Peshwas also had their own family rivalries and tensions.

Other sibling rivalries in the medieval era included the Rajput kings Sawai Jai Singh of Amber and his brother Bijay Singh in 1600s.

Mir Jafar and his son in law Mir Qasim, nawabs of Bengal also had a family rivalry during the 1700s.

1.5 Family property disputes in the British era

After the British came to India and established their rule over the whole of India, wars between kings became much less, but property disputes between siblings continued as always. This too was at all levels and all strata of society including between Zamindars and small farmers and princely states and industrialists. British established courts such as the high court of Calcutta had to deal with a number of property disputes.

1.6 Family property disputes in independent India

After independence, India has also seen a number of property disputes within joint families. A few of the ones involving famous people such as politicians and industrialists are well known.

A well-known recent example is the squabble between the Ambani brothers, Anil and Mukesh, upon the death of their father Dhirubhai Ambani in 2002, founder of the Reliance group and arguably the richest family in India. The fight was about how best to divide up the huge conglomerate among the brothers. After a few years of the feud, a truce was finally brokered by their mother Kokilaben in 2005, leading to the split of the Reliance group among the brothers.

Similar problems between siblings have been seen in the Hinduja brothers. A similar fight happened between the Godrej brothers, owners of the Godrej conglomerate comprising consumers products and other brands. Another such split was within the real estate developers Hiranandani family. There were also inter family disputes in the family of Singhanias, owners of Raymond fashion retailers, steel magnates Kirloskar brothers, the Mafatlals and a few others.

1.7 Conclusion

To conclude, we can see that property disputes among family members in India is by no means a recent phenomenon. It has been part of Indian history since the most ancient times and medieval times all the way to the modern era.

CHAPTER TWO

Psychology of Sibling Rivalries Leading to Property Disputes

In this chapter we discuss the psychology behind family rivalries, in particular the most common form which is the rivalry between siblings. Brothers and sisters usually grow up together and there is competition for the parents' and other family members' attention. On top of it, brothers keep on getting compared to each other, especially in terms of achievements, by the rest of society. This creates a sense of rivalry and jealousy, which may manifest later in life in things such as property disputes. There might also be feelings of entitlement and victimization by one or more siblings, feelings that they have been unjustly treated by their parents and so on.

We first discuss a few psychology theories related to developmental and family psychology. Our aim is to understand how sibling rivalries develop over time.

2.1 Freud's theory of development

As per the psychosocial theory of development by Sigmund Freud and other psychologists, many or most of our problems stem from our childhood. Our mind has three aspects: the conscious mind that we are aware of, the subconscious and the unconscious mind which has latent or hidden impulses. Accordingly, the experiences we have had as children shape our view of the world.

As per Freud's theory, there is a constant interplay between three factors in our mind: id, ego and superego. Of these, the Id is driven by basic and primal instinctual needs such as pleasure and hunger, not considering the needs of others. This is predominant in babies, who cry when their needs are not being fulfilled. The ego is more balanced, considers the reality of each situation and balances our own needs with those of others in the world. The superego is the voice of our conscience and morality and typically also develops later in life. So in cases where the ego, id and superego are not balanced from an early age, a person may grow to have psychological issues later in life, including issues with their siblings.

2.2 Melanie Klein's Object Relations Theory

Melanie Klein was a developmental psychologist who came after Freud. She developed a theory of relationships called object relations theory, such as between a mother and a child. As per the theory, the child projects good and bad, love and hate feelings upon separate parts of its mother, depending on whether their needs are being met and to what extent.

David Wincott, another developmental psychologist, further developed Klein's theory and suggested that psychological difficulties develop during the baby's growth if the environment, including the mother, fail to satisfy their needs on a regular and reliable basis.

2.3 John Bowlby's Attachment Theory

As per the theory of attachment postulated by the developmental psychologist John Bowlby, the relationship of the child with their mother is essential to how they develop later in life. The quality and nature of the bond with the mother, and how the child is cared for in their early years, is crucial in forming the child's world view. If their initial experiences are positive and they have the feeling of being loved, they will develop a healthy and secure view of the world. If their initial experiences are of being unloved, their view of the world will be similar.

2.4 Systemic Therapy and Structural Family Therapy

A number of psychologists in the 1960s, especially in the Palo Alto Mental Research Institute, postulated the idea of systemic therapy. Their main idea was that communication of members within the family and other social circles is most important. Later problems in one's individual psychology can be traced to one's social relationships, such as within the family and one's social circle. The language used in communication within the family define the values and relationships.

For example, lots of friction and quarreling between the adults in the family, such as one's parents, may cause the children to themselves become disruptive at school or later in life. Hence, by understanding this and altering the interactions between family members to more healthy interactions, we can create conditions for a healthier development of the children within the family.

The theory of Structural Family Therapy emerged from these. This states that dynamics, power relations and boundaries within the family shape the individuals' psychological development. How the parents enforce the rules and boundaries for their kids, how the rules and family hierarchy is structured, how the family copes with difficult external situations, are all important factors.

For example, a child can learn in a family that the more they are disruptive, the more attention they get from their parents. This may end up in later life their developing into narcissist and psychopathic individuals when they grow up, not caring for the feelings of others and doing whatever it takes to meet their aims in their corporate career or in terms of getting hold of property within the family.

The later Milan School of psychologists further developed the theories of family therapy. They postulated that the values and communication within the family are very important. Meaning is created through the family values and communication, and it is a dynamic and changing process.

2.5 Psychology of sibling rivalries in India

From the above theories, we can understand that a lot of the roots of the sibling rivalries, which later manifest into property disputes, may emerge from an early age, from relationships and dynamics within the family, especially the relationships of the siblings with their parents. In the families where the parents make an effort to consciously maintain a healthy relationship between siblings, such rivalries are less likely to happen. But if the family does not have established mechanisms for resolving problems and disputes within family members, this might lead to issues.

Unfortunately, in places like India, where there are limited resources and too much competition, such healthy trends are less likely to occur in families. Children in the family, especially brothers, are constantly compared to each other and even compared with the achievements of their parents, not only by their parents but also by other relatives and wider society. This creates an unhealthy environment where there is too much expectation and pressure on the kids.

Added to this can be the problem of favoritism by parents to one sibling compared to another. The resultant rivalry and jealousy a kid may have towards their own brothers and sisters when growing up may result into bad relations and disputes later on.

CHAPTER THREE

Statistics of Property Related Court Cases in India

Property dispute and land dispute related court cases are the longest pending and the highest number (about 66%) clogging the Indian court system. A significant number of these property disputes are likely to be within the same family, however the exact numbers are not known.

In this chapter we focus on the scale of property disputes in Indian courts, in terms of numbers of such court cases and time taken to resolve the cases.

Property and land disputes are bad for all parties involved. They lead to high litigation costs with no productive results, and are a burden on the economy. Sometimes the property disputes take decades or even generations to resolve. Often, they are related to inheritance and succession within the same family, in which case they further lead to bad blood within the family. Such disputes affect all classes of people: even the richest families of industrialists are not immune to them.

3.1 Data on the scale of property disputes in India

A 2016 newspaper article, based on a study by Daksh, mentioned that land and property cases account for two thirds of all pending civil court cases in India, including 7.5 million civil cases. Total cost of such litigation was 0.5% of India's GDP.

Another report by Center for policy research (CPR) found the following:

- Property disputes affect around 7.7 million people in India.
- Property disputes clog every level of courts in India from district and lower courts to supreme court.
- Property disputes are the largest both in terms of absolute numbers and time taken to resolve the cases.

- About 25% of all cases decided by the Supreme Court involve property disputes.
- Property disputes make up 66% of all civil cases in India.
- The average time taken to resolve a property dispute, from creation of the dispute to resolution by the Supreme Court, is 20 years.

3.2 Types of property cases in Indian courts

Property and land disputes encompass a wide variety of cases in Indian courts. These can include the following types of cases:

- Cases related to succession and inheritance within the family (especially concerning the Hindu Succession Act 1925) encompass a good percentage of the pending property cases in Indian courts.
- Property cases related to registration of land records: Some of the property cases occur when a buyer buys some property and finds out it is not registered properly with the land authorities or municipal authorities by the previous owners.
- Property cases due to fraud and other crimes: Some of the ongoing property cases may be related to fraudulent transactions, such as when a person has been fraudulently deprived of their rightful claim on the land or property.
- Property cases due to tenancy: Some of the cases may be due to a tenant refusing to vacate their land when their tenancy period has expired.
- Property cases due to trespassing or illegal occupation.

3.3 Reasons for the huge number of property disputes

There are multiple reasons for the huige number of pending property cases in Indian courts. One problem is lots of exceptions in the law and the complexities of the cases. There are a number of laws related to inheritance, such as Indian Succession act, 1925. There are different variances in the succession laws for Muslims and Christians and Hindus.

There are also a number of exceptions and special clauses in various laws, for example in states like Uttaranchal, Himachal Pradesh and North East, where only people who are domiciled are allowed to own land.

This creates a situation where there are too many laws and a common man has no choice but to take the help of expensive lawyers and court cases to enforce their property rights using the applicable laws.

References

1. Thomas Reuters, Deccan Chronicle. Millions of land, property cases stuck in courts. August 2016. Available: https://www.deccanchronicle.com/nation/current-affairs/090816/millions-of-land-property-cases-stuck-in-indian-courts.html

2. Namita Wahi, Center for Policy Research. Understanding Land Conflict in India and Suggestions for Reform. June 2019. Available: https://cprindia.org/news/7922

3. Arunav Kaul, Ahmed Pathan, Harish Narasappa. Daksh report. Deconstructing Delay: Analyses of Data from High Courts and Subordinate Courts. Available: https://dakshindia.org/Daksh_Justice_in_India/19_chapter_01.xhtml

CHAPTER FOUR

Law Related to Succession of Property in India

In this chapter we discuss the main law related to succession and property transfer in India. The main law related to succession is called the Indian Succession Act 1925, which governs the transfer of moveable as well as immoveable property through inheritance or succession upon one's death. It was made in British Indian in 1925, but some subsequent amendments have since been made to the law.

4.1 Indian Succession Act 1925

The Indian Succession Act 1925 is an act to consolidate the law applicable to intestate (dying without a will) and testamentary succession (succession where a will is present). The purpose of this law is to present the whole body of statutory law on the subject of wills and succession in a complete form.

The ordinary meaning of the word "succession" is a transmission by law or by the will of the man to one or more persons of the property and transmission rights and obligations of a deceased person. The federal court gave its opinion on a reference in the matter of the powers of the federal legislature to provide for the levy of an estate duty in respect of property other than agricultural land, passing upon the death of any person [AIR 1944 FC 73].

THE INDIAN SUCCESSION ACT, 1925

ACT NO. 39 OF 1925[1]

[30*th September*, 1925.]

An Act to consolidate the law applicable to intestate and testamentary succession [2]***.

WHEREASit is expedient to consolidate the law applicable to intestate and testamentary succession [2]***. It is hereby enacted as follows:—

PART I

PRELIMINARY

1. Short title.—This Act may be called the Indian Succession Act, 1925.

2. Definitions.—In this Act, unless there is anything repugnant in the subject or context,—

(*a*) "administrator" means a person appointed by competent authority to administer the estate of a deceased person when there is no executor;

(*b*) "codicil" means an instrument made in relation to a Will, and explaining, altering or adding to its dispositions, and shall be deemed to form part of the Will;

[3][(*bb*) "District Judge" means the Judge of a Principal Civil Court of original jurisdiction;]

(*c*) "executor" means a person to whom the execution of the last Will of a deceased person is, by the testator's appointment, confided;

[4][(*cc*) "India" means the territory of India excluding the State of Jammu and Kashmir;]

(*d*) "Indian Christian" means a native of India who is, or in good faith claims to be, of unmixed Asiatic descent and who professes any form of the Christian religion;

Figure: First page of the Indian Succession Act 1925

The law of succession is the law governing the transmission of property vested in a person at his death to some other person or persons.

The act discusses the cases in which a person can die with or without making a will:

- A person dies intestate i.e. without making a will, and how their moveable and immoveable property can be divided among their various heirs starting from the closest relatives such as widow and children.
- Testamentary succession, i.e. where the deceased person has left a will before they died, specifying exactly how their property can be divided and among whom.

4.2 Summary of the Indian succession act

The Indian succession act covers different grounds related to wills and other aspects of succession.

It discusses who can and cannot make a will, what is a valid will, different types of bequests, how an administrator can be appointed, how probate and letters of succession can be granted, how debts, legacies and gifts are to be paid and so on. It also covers different state amendments.

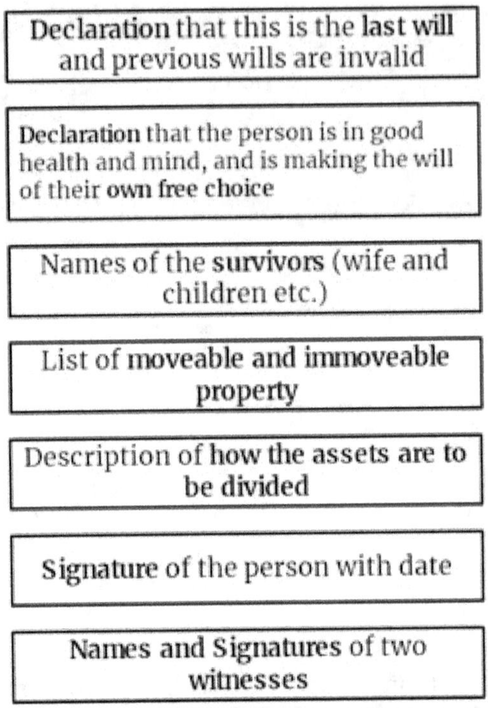

Figure: The main components of a will

4.3 Characteristics of a will as per Indian Succession Act

The essential characteristics of a will are as follows:

- There must be a legal declaration of the testator's (the person making the will) intention
- The declaration must be with respect to the property of the testator
- The declaration must be to the effect that it is to operate after the death of the testator i.e. it should be revocable during the life of the testator.
- It lists the moveable and immoveable assets and states how and among whom the assets are to be divided and in what ratio
- The will must be signed and attested by two witnesses

4.4 Things to keep in mind while making arrangements for succession of one's property

Following are some important financial and legal aspects one should keep in mind related to arrangements for their property after one's death:

The choice for a person making arrangements for succession of one's property is between leaving a will or dying intestate. A valid will ensures that a testator can determine what happens to our property after his death. If one does not make a will, i.e. one dies intestate, the law of the state will determine how one's property will be distributed to whom and in what proportions and the person has no choice in the matter. Without a will, assets and belongings will be distributed on death according to the law of intestacy. The intestacy laws benefit blood relatives in the order of proximity, but charities and close friends get nothing.

In order to prepare one's will, one needs to approach a solicitor. Any solicitor can prepare a will. The solicitor fees can vary from as less as Rs 50000 to 200000 depending on the following factors:

- Size of the estate
- The complexity of the will itself

It is advisable to confirm in advance with the solicitor how much would be the legal cost. Alternatively, a person may choose not to use a solicitor and draft a will by himself. Similarly, a person may choose whether to register his will at the sub-registrar's office or not.

The things to keep in mind after drafting one's will are as follows:

- Once a will is executed (written, signed and attested by two witnesses) it takes a legal form.
- It can then be kept in a safe place by the testator, to be opened after his or her death.
- It can also be kept at a sub registrar's office (what is called a "registered will") for safety and record keeping.
- Note: Since the will may not be seen till after the funeral is over, it is a good idea to tell one's family and proposed executors about one's wishes in terms of the manner of one's funeral and organ donation, since this cannot be delayed
- A person may, before one's death, tell one's family members that he or she has signed a will and deposited for safekeeping in a probate court or

bank

When someone dies, the partner or close relatives have to deal with a multitude of practical matters as well as coping with their emotions. In the short term:

(i) the death must be registered,

(ii) arrangements should be made for the funeral,

(iii) the immediate day to day expenses of the dependents must be provided for, after which the affairs of the deceased person must be settled.

This means someone must take charge of his/her property, personal possessions, debts, business and so forth, which the law calls by the term "the deceased's estate".

No charge is to be levied for a medical certificate if the death was due to natural causes. One must register the death within five days with the concerned Registrar of births, marriages and deaths. The death is recorded in a register of deaths and a certified copy of the entry is called "the death certificate". Several copies of the death certificate need to be prepared for use in different places.

Arranging for the funeral: Funeral directors should provide one with the price lists and written estimates. Whoever arranges the funeral is responsible for payment. If the deceased left enough assets or cash, one may be able to claim reimbursement out of the estate for reasonable funeral expenses.

Joint bank account: Personal accounts are frozen on death. Joint accounts can be operated provided that both the account holders are not required to sign every cheque. One can operate a joint account provided it needs a single signature.

The deceased's affairs:

(a) The deceased's papers: in order to find out of there is a will, one needs to go through the personal papers left by the deceased, check with his or her bank along with the past and present solicitors whether they hold his will. It might also have been deposited in the safe custody of the registry.

(b) Bank direct debits and standing orders / credit cards: One should check all direct debit mandates and standing orders. These cease on death if paid through a bank account in the deceased's sole name. One should make sure that all credit cards are returned with notice of death to the card companies, in order to avoid fraudulent misuse.

(c) The personnel representatives who are the official representatives of the deceased to take charge of an estate:

To take charge of the deceased's property

To pay outstanding debts and taxes

To ascertain which persons are entitled to what is left

To ensure that beneficiaries are given their proper share

(d) A word of caution: if one deals with any property of a deceased person without any authority to do so, one can be liable to penalties.

4.5 Format of a sample will

The format of a sample will is as follows:

I, <name of testator>, son of <father's name>, aged <age in years>, resident of <address of testator>, declare this to be my last will and testament. This will cancels all my prior wills made by me.

I am in good health and possess a good mind. This will was made independently by me. No one has influenced or compelled me to make this will.

I hereby appoint <name of executor>, as the sole executor of this will.

My wife's name is <name of wife>. We have <number of children> children, whose names are as follows:

1.

2.

I have the following immovable and movable property:

1. A flat in the address ____

2. Jewelry, shares in various companies, cash and cash in bank accounts.

I declare that all the above assets are owned by me, and I have full authority over these assets.

I entrust all my movable and immovable properties to the following persons in the following ways

1. I give my bank account to my wife

2. I give my flat in the name of my son

( )

Testator's signature

Date

Signed by the testator as a last will in our presence. We have fully understood and approved the material and have signed our names as witnesses in the presence of the testator and in the presence of each other.

Name and signature of witnesses:

1.(name and signature of witness)

2. (name and signature of witness)

CHAPTER FIVE

Law Related to Transfer of Property in India

The main law related to transfer of property between living persons in India is called Transfer of Property Act, which consolidates the law in India related to property transfers. The act was made in British India in 1882 and has survived in independent India with a few modifications.

THE TRANSFER OF PROPERTY ACT, 1882

ACT NO. 4 OF 1882

[*17th February*, 1882.]

An Act to amend the law relating to the Transfer of Property by act of Parties.

Preamble.—WHEREAS it is expedient to define and amend certain parts of the law relating to the transferof property by act of parties; It is hereby enacted as follows:—

CHAPTER I

PRELIMINARY

1. **Short title.**—This Act may becalled the Transfer of Property Act, 1882.

Commencement.—It shallcome into force on the first day of July, 1882.

Extent.—[1][Itextends[2] in the first instance to the whole of India, except [3][the territories which, immediately before the 1st November, 1956, were comprised in Part B States or in the States of], Bombay, Punjab and Delhi.]

[4][But this Act or any part thereof may by [5]notification in the Official Gazette be extended to the whole or any part of [6][the said territories] by the State Government concerned.]

[7][And any State Government may, [8]*** from time to time, by notification in the Official Gazette, exempt, either retrospectively or prospectively, any part of the territories administered by such State Government from all or any of the following provisions, namely:—

Sections 54, paragraphs 2 and 3, 59, 107 and 123.]

Figure: First page of the Transfer of Property Act 1882

5.1 Introduction to the Transfer of Property Act

The Transfer of Property Act states the conditions and procedure following which a property can get transferred from one person to another. It discusses the different modes of transfer of property including sales, mortgages, leases, exchange and gifts.

In this act, property refers to both moveable as well as immoveable property. Transfer of property, according to the act, is defined as conveying a property to himself or another living person, including a company or group of individuals, in present or future. The rights, interest, ownership and/or possession of the property can be transferred.

As per the act, any person who is mentally competent and fulfills the other conditions for making a contract can transfer property to another, provided they own the property or are authorized to transfer it. They can transfer it orally or in writing, themselves or by hiring a competent lawyer.

5.2 Conditions for the transfer of property under Transfer of Property Act

The conditions for transfer are as follows:

- The transfer must be between two living persons
- The property being transferred should be transferable. It should not have any circumstances in which it cannot be transferred, such as chance of a heir apparent succeeding to an estate. It should not be a common asset belonging to all, such as the air or sea, that cannot be transferred.
- The person making the transfer should own the property or be competent to transfer it.
- The transfer should be done via a valid method such as sale, exchange, mortgage, lease or gift.
- The transfer cannot be in opposition to the rule of perpetuity. E.g. there should be no condition in the transfer that occurs after infinite time or the lifetime of any of the persons involved.

5.3 Types of Transfers Under Transfer of Property Act

The Transfer of Property act describes different ways in which property can be transferred. For each of these, it describes the transfer and the rights and duties of the parties to the transfer.

The different types of transfer described in the Transfer of Property act are as follows:

- Sale of property: Sale means a transfer of ownership upon a price paid or promised.
- Mortgage of immoveable property: This refers to the transfer of interest in immoveable property as a security for a loan. The act contains detailed

instructions on the rights and liabilities of a mortgager and mortgagee, how the mortgage can be redeemed, issues such as foreclosure of a mortgage, how a receiver can be appointed and so on.

- Lease of immoveable property: This is the transfer of the rights to enjoy a property for a specified time and upon regular payment of an amount or rent.
- Exchange: This is when two persons mutually transfer the ownership of one thing for another or for money only, it is called an exchange.
- Gift: Gift is the transfer of moveable or immoveable property by one party, called the donor, to another party called the donee, voluntarily and without any consideration, and accepted by the donee party.
- Actionable claim: Transfer of actionable claim means transfer of property upon a claim such as debt, from the debtor to the one they are in debt to, or who has a legally enforceable claim against them.

For each of the above types of transfers, the act lays down the procedure and defines the rights and liabilities of the parties to the transfer.

CHAPTER SIX

Procedure for Fighting Property Court Cases

A property court case, as we have seen earlier, typically takes several years in Indian courts. The initial case may be filed at the district court or some lower court. In case of an unfavorable verdict, some of the parties may appeal in higher courts such as the high court or supreme court.

Most family related property court cases are succession related i.e. when the patriarch or matriarch of the family has died leaving some property and the children are fighting to divide it among themselves. In that case, they may be related to a will, if it exists, or multiple copies of the will, or in some cases there may be no will at all. Most of such cases would be governed under the Indian Succession Act and would be related to getting a probate or letters of administration of the will. Even within will related succession court cases, there may be a variety: cases related to moveable property left in the will, immoveable property, or both.

There might also be family cases related to other things than succession, for example if the patriarch is old but not died yet and the sons are fighting over who will manage the assets of the family business.

6.1 Court Procedure for probate and other property cases

The court procedure for probating a will generally includes the following steps:

Submission: Petitioners file the probate application at the court in the prescribed format, along with original copies of the will, death certificate, affidavit and court fees.

Verification: Court receives the probate application and verifies details.

Publication: Court directs to publish in newspapers a notice inviting members of the public and next of kin to file objections. It also directs to send notification letters to the next of kin to appear in the court.

Issuance: If there is no objection, the court issues the probate and letters of administration.

Upon Objection: If there is an objection, the normal court procedure takes place. This includes filing of arguments and evidence, cross examination etc. After examining evidence and arguments, the court issues its judgment regarding the grant of probate.

For property cases other than probate of a will, a similar procedure is applicable, except that parts related to the will are not used.

In the following subsections we share some important things to keep in mind when fighting the cases.

6.2 Choosing a good lawyer for fighting the court cases

One important strategy for court cases is to get a good and competent lawyer whom we can trust to fight the court cases.

One should engage a lawyer who is competent and has prior experience in dealing with such cases in his or her career. We should make sure the lawyer keeps themselves abreast of current knowledge in law including recent judgments, is comfortable with technology such as email and remote hearings. Considering that remote hearings and e-filings have become more common nowadays with the Covid-19 pandemic and are here to stay even after the pandemic is over, we should make sure that the lawyer too should be comfortable with this.

The most important quality in a good lawyer is that they should listen to the client and be ready to act as per the client's instructions. They should not have the attitude that they know better than the client, or that they always know what is best and their decisions cannot be questions. The best lawyers are usually humble, open minded and respect the fact that the client knows best about his or her own case.

6.3 Managing one's lawyer

We should try to skillfully manage the lawyer during the conduct of the case, including negotiating the fees in advance, giving proper incentives and so on. We should also try to be friendly with the lawyer and not pick up fights with them over petty issues. If we decide to change the lawyer, we should try to do so amicably and without fighting.

6.4 Changing one's lawyer

One should not be attached to any one lawyer and be ready to change one's lawyer if the need arises, for example if the current lawyer is no longer able to effectively represent our case.

The normal procedure is to file a new "wakalatnama" for the new lawyer at the court, stating that this lawyer will be representing this case from now on.

As per the Indian laws, the existing lawyer cannot stop any client from changing their lawyer, even if they do not provide a “No Objection Certificate”.

Having said that, it is also not a good practice to change lawyers too frequently during the case. Having chosen a lawyer, we should not have undue expectations on them and give them some time to prove themselves. We should also try to be amicable while changing the lawyer.

6.5 Handling finances for fighting the case

An important part of any court case is handling one’s finances properly. If not properly planned and budgeted in advance, the costs including the lawyer’s fees, cost of hiring new lawyers, cost of filing additional cases, travel related to cases etc. may spiral out of control.

Therefore, it is important to first estimate the budget by asking our friends and acquaintances who have dealt with similar cases. We can also research on the internet or on forums such as lawrato.com where one can get advice from lawyers on specific aspects of the law.

Having estimated our budget for the case, we should figure out how to arrange our finances to pay for it. We should also take into account that the case can drag for a longer time and may lead to multiple related cases rather than just a single case. Even if we cannot estimate a fixed number given all kinds of varying costs, we should budget for a certain approximate sum every year the case runs,

In times when we have to make finance related decisions, such as if our lawyer advises us to file an additional case or go for a strategy that costs us money, we should do a proper cost benefit analysis before deciding to allocate extra funds.

The same goes for how to pay the lawyer’s fees. We should negotiate paying them in installments rather than the entire fee at once, and also make it dependent on how long the case runs.

6.6 The art of cross examination

Sometimes, we may be cross examined by the opposite party, during the conduct of the case. Or else, we may have to advise our own lawyer on how to cross examine the opposite party and what questions to ask them. It is important to prepare properly for such an eventuality. We should act as our own devil’s advocate and prepare a list of questions as well as the opposite party's probable answers to all such questions. We should even practice the cross-examination session with a friend or simply in front of a mirror. We should not take it lightly but try our best to give the prepared answers as per our strategy so as not to weaken our case. Similarly, we should prepare the questions for the opposite party based on a close analysis of their position and how best to weaken their case. We should go over the questions carefully with our lawyer beforehand.

CHAPTER SEVEN

Conclusion

In this book, we have gone through the phenomenon of property disputes in India within the family. we have briefly gone through the history and psychology of such disputes, as well as the legal aspects of the same.

About The Authors

Siva Prasad Bose is an author of various introductory guidebooks related to aspects of Indian laws. He is currently retired after many years of service in Uttar Pradesh Power Corporation Limited. He received his engineering degree from Jadavpur University, Kolkata and has a law degree from Meerut University, Meerut. His interests lie in the fields of family law, civil law, law of contracts, and areas of law related to power grid and electricity revenue related issues.

Joy Bose is a software engineer and a data scientist by profession.

About The Author

Other Books By Siva Prasad Bose

Introduction to Wills and Probate
Senior Citizens Abuse in India
Introduction to negotiable instruments
Introduction to marriage laws in India
Neighbor Problems in India and what to do about them
Managing Court Cases with Mental Strength
Delays in Court Cases in India
Introduction to Patents and Patent Law in India

www.ingramcontent.com/pod-product-compliance
Lightning Source LLC
LaVergne TN
LVHW022325200926
848481LV00004B/1439
9798886298390